The

Eidetic

Afterlife

Hypothesis

a reinterpretation of death and dying

The

Eidetic Afterlife

Hypothesis

(a reinterpretation of death and dying)

a multidimensional exploration

by J. Martin Strangeweather

Cover art by J. Martin Strangeweather

Printed in the United States of America

Published by the Santa Ana Literary Association

ISBN: 979-8-218-34165-7

"Mind = Matter" and "Focus" first appeared in *Sophoetics: Philosophy Poems* (Finishing Line Press 2023)

"Hamster Wheel" and "Tears of Osiris: A Recipe for Disaster" first appeared in *Poems from the Polka-Dot Apocalypse* (Four Feathers Press 2021)

This book is dedicated to a more unified

understanding of humanity.

FOREWORD

Whether the reader of this book is living or dying, the ideas herein are worthy of consideration, as the topic touches all. There have been many treatises on death, yet probably none as daring or motley as this which you now hold in your hand.

In this book, an assemblage of poems and non-poems or un-poems be they prose, aphorism, or postulate, Strangeweather guides the reader into accepting a uniquely forged take on life and death, dreams, pre-life, post-life.

He states that life, as death, is determined by the beliefs of the individual and that we exist, have always existed in the domain of starless darkness. One might venture to call it proto-galactic cosmos. And therein do we return. The concept naturally lends itself to poetical exploration… and to Kierkegaard: "Life can only be understood backward but must be lived forward." So what are we doing here and how do we do "Life"? This book concludes that our only recourse is to cherish love and contact with others, to savor pain, to confront our fears, and relish every beat of the heart.

But don't take my word for it. Read on. Expand your mind. And mind what you put in your mind. The mind is a stomach and information is nutrition. Conversely, the stomach is also a mind.

Take the back seat, Robert Anton Wilson. Within these pages you will find a historical summary of the Soul as conceived by ancient philosophers, an examination of the shortcomings of Christianity, and a musical number between Mephistopheles and Dr. Faustus.

This book is an alternative walkthrough on life, death, the Soul, and a reexamination of the function and necessity of God and religion filtered through the marvelous mind of the modern Dr. Faustus, neo-bard for the end times, J. Martin Strangeweather.

— Youssef Alaoui, author of *Critics of Mystery Marvel*

We live and die in the same breath. The coffin looms over us, dark and gargantuan, taller than a skyscraper, bigger than a mountain, vaster than the entire world and all of human history, vaster than time, and imminently more concrete. But the coffin was made by a mortal's own hand. It was constructed to appear a certain way, to embody a certain set of concepts, facilitating and fulfilling certain sociological, psychological, and spiritual functions.

Hamster Wheel

All the movies have already been watched.
All the amusement park rides
Have already been ridden.

The races have all been run.
The products have all been bought
And sold.

All the backs have been stabbed.
All the books have been written.
All the words . . . spoken.
All the thoughts . . . thought.

Hamster wheel,
Hamster wheel,
Remember a time before stars.
You are not these things.
You are nothing more than these things.

But what could this mean?

Your chair is made of eggshells,
Your bed is made of salted wounds,
Dresser full of Freudian slips and
Secondhand dreams,
Uniforms fashioned from broken mirrors,
None of which reflect you,
While the clock whispers lies.

All the lives have already been lived.
All the gods have already been invented.

Hamster wheel galaxy
In the fractal multi-lingua-verse,
Spin me a web
To call home.

To imagine something is to trick our state of consciousness into mimicking the state we would experience if we perceived it. To remember something is to trick our current state of consciousness into mimicking the experience of a prior state. To empathize with something is to imagine its state of consciousness and take it upon oneself.

Memory can only recreate a small portion of any given prior experience. If memory could recreate the entirety of any given prior experience, that would be considered a form of time travel.

Mind = Matter

Everything is information.

Everything is mind.

Your brain is processing information.

Your brain is processing mind.

Subtract your eyesight.

Subtract your hearing.

Subtract your sense of smell, taste, and touch.

Subtract your ability to move.

Subtract your ability to think.

Subtract your ability to remember.

Subtract all your abilities to process information.

What is left over?

Unprocessed information.

Unprocessed mind.

Mind unfettered.

Focus

Focus on a chair.

Any chair will suffice.

The chair is not outside your mind.

The chair is not inside your mind.

The chair is your mind.

Now focus on love.

Focus on divinity.

Any divinity will suffice.

You have a concept of life that you correlate with a concept of death that you correlate with a concept of afterlife that you correlate with a concept of justice that you correlate with a concept of truth that you correlate with a concept of identity that you correlate with a concept of history that you correlate with a concept of memory that you correlate with a concept of mind that you correlate with a concept of brain that you correlate with a concept of body that you correlate with a concept of physicality that you correlate with a concept of physics that you correlate with a concept of math that you correlate with a concept of proof that you correlate with a concept of belief, and so on . . .

Death is manmade. Death is a concept.

The passage of time is malleable. American neuroscientist Hudson Hoagland (born: 1899 AD, died: 1982 AD) discovered that time is more than just relative to position and momentum—there is a completely different gauge of time inherent to each individual: interoceptive temporality, or psychophysiological time. Interoceptive temporality is a subjective underlying feeling of time based on physiological factors (such as temperature) and psychological factors (such as stress). Each of us views life through an individualized psychophysiological time-lens controlled by our body's internal chemistry. This time-sense can be distorted and even manipulated by altering the body's temperature or its ability to utilize oxygen. The brain relies on its own autonomic rhythms to measure the duration of a moment and the span of events. Mr. Hoagland, studying sick patients, determined that the heightened temperature arising from fever causes a subsequent acceleration of the sense of temporal sequences. Higher temperatures make our cerebral clocks run faster, thereby shortening our perception of time's passage. Hoagland later realized that restricting the brain's oxygen flow also has the effect of speeding up the sensation of time. As people grow older and become less capable of taking in and processing oxygen, many of them begin to experience the years passing more rapidly. Our minds actually do observe time to move at a faster rate during the elderly stage of life due to oxygen depletion. The perception of time can be shortened to the feeling that every moment is flying by, or it can be elongated to feel as if every moment is crawling in slow motion—the data-processors of our brains can be sped up or slowed down by various biological, chemical, and psychosocial factors. Bottom line, the perception of time can be altered.

There is a hyper-dilation of dream time during the dying process, when certain regions of the brain responsible for our perception of temporal sequences begin to shut down.

Most of us have never seen a ghost or alien. Most of us have never conversed with an angel or been tempted by a devil (in the literal sense), and none of us has ever breathed underwater or levitated . . . except in our dreams.

Life is the wavering flame of the candle, and eternity lies within the brief moments of a dream. Each human spends their lifetime—their *waking* lifetime—being conditioned as to what they will experience (dream? hallucinate?) during their final living moments. The dreamer rarely knows they are in a dream when they are in a dream (lucid dreams being the exception). Triggered by overwhelmingly traumatic events (such as dying), the eternity of heaven, hell, nirvana, or anyplace else may be the product of a powerful dream/hallucination that occurs hours, minutes, or even seconds before death.

Eternity is not out there somewhere. Our afterlife hides within each one of us, and through synaptic overload and the release of various neurochemicals, eternity is conjured in the few moments preceding death as opposed to afterward. This is a working hypothesis, not a religion. While the hypothesis attempts to sidestep the debate between atheism, agnosticism, and theism, its transformative effect on each of these standpoints cannot be overlooked.

Before religion . . . before philosophy and science. . .
we dreamed. And we shared our dreams. Dreams are
a universal experience among humans. In ancient
times, whenever a tribesperson ceased to move and
breathe, the rest of the tribe/family considered them
to be dreaming in a deep slumber from which they
would never awake.*

*Ancient conceptions of dreaming tend to be more
reverent than our contemporary interpretation of the
experience.

Time becomes indecipherable in the lightless vacuum of a black hole. Question: How does time pass in the imagination? Answer: It doesn't. In a dream state, time passes according to the whims of imagination, making temporal sequences arbitrary and unaccountable to the linear progression of clock time (i.e., external-world chronometrical increments denoting the sequential permutation of objects and their interrelationships). We know the perception of time can be altered. People on their deathbed are known to vividly recall childhood memories long since forgotten and often experience nonlinear temporal hallucinations, reliving scenes from their history in a random, confused order. Let us not forget the overused trope: "My whole life flashed before my eyes." The effects of drugs and alcohol have also been proven to skewer the sense of time. Similarly, extreme moods can affect our experience of time's passage.

If time is relative (which indeed it is), and the perception of time were altered enough, could a second be made to feel like a hundred years? And if a hundred years, why not the possibility of stretching the feeling to a thousand years, or even a million? The duration of any given moment is eidetic. Could a perceived eternity be hammered out of any moment if the perception of time were made malleable enough? Everyone knows a dream can seem just as real as our experience of waking reality (for example: wet dreams and nightmares). Our sense of time is recalibrated, re-temporalized, every morning upon awakening back into the world of schedules, sunsets, and seasons, but what if we never awoke? What would happen if the waking world's influence of clock time and mortal linearity were completely unavailable to us as reference points from which to arrange the order of our perceived moments?

Heaven is located in the mind of the believer, and so is hell. Neurobiologists have noted that the human brain, when undergoing the final stage of the dying process, releases an array of endorphins. These neurochemical secretions cause dreams and hallucinations. They can act as stimulants, depressants, and opiates, producing different states of being ranging from euphoria to sexual ecstasy to utter horror, and seemingly limitless combinations thereof. In your particular worldline the effects of these neurochemicals are not yet fully understood and accounted for, but a small number of researchers have conjectured that during the final churning of the brain's most mysterious elixirs, one's uniquely conditioned (tailor-made) afterlife is "dreamt up." Note, there has never been a grouping of humans that did not have some form of ingrained afterlife concept/bias, even if it was one of non-existence.

Thus, it is within the quick spark of living that the groundwork for infinity is laid, and without running afoul of paradox, eternity could exist in the shallow span of a nanosecond.

Death is relative. You will never experience the moment of your death. In a very real sense, you will never die.

Infinity and timelessness are different concepts that often get confused for one another.

Perhaps the most infinitesimal moment between functionality (life) and total system shutdown (death) ends up in a superpositional state of quantum indeterminacy.

The womb from which religion is born could very well turn out to be a subtle misapprehension of visions produced by an oversaturation of carbon dioxide, a surge of synaptic activity, and the bombardment of various neurochemicals during extremely traumatic events such as near-death experiences and the final stage of dying. However, the hypothesis of a dreamed afterlife is in no way meant to invalidate or replace mainstream systems of spirituality. The dreamed afterlife hypothesis simply avoids metaphysical issues altogether. Inverting the popular conception of life after death into a pre-death experience has many beneficial consequences in the "real" world, not the least of which is cultural unification. The understanding that each of us dreams our own specific afterlife promotes fellowship and tolerance among all religions. We are all fellow dreamers, though our dreams may differ.

The dreamed afterlife hypothesis leads to a unique system of ethics not reliant on the dictates of a hypothetical otherworldly authority. Instead, each one of us holds ourselves directly accountable. This means total responsibility is assumed in every action of every waking moment. There are no rhetorical stratagems to ease you of the horror, shame, and despair you create during your life's journey. You are your own judge, and you cannot deceive yourself. No amount of "Hail Marys" will rid you of the guilt that was never honestly resolved. Ego defense mechanisms acquired in the waking world to fool yourself into contentment will be of no use during your last breath. Dreams have a will of their own to drudge up things forgotten or suppressed.

The dream variation of the afterlife concept is user friendly and impartial. Its very foundation (your memories and thoughts) demands complete accountability unto yourself. You will definitely die, and quite possibly before this event, you will be subjected to everything you ever felt, sensed, thought, and did—everything your subconscious/unconscious database ever stored—perfect and inescapable justice. "Organic" justice. Neurological research suggests the human brain is capable of storing approximately 300 years' worth of television programming, which is odd for a creature that rarely lives past 80. Be mindful of what you fill your psyche with.

We will all become characters in one another's dreams. How will you be visualized? Interesting moral considerations arise from the hypothesis of the dreamed afterlife. If you want to dream of a peaceful hereafter, you would be wise to live out your days peacefully in peaceful environments. If you spend your short life in toil, strife, and anxiety, then heaven help you in the nightmarish eternity that awaits. None of us wish to relive painful situations, so we should be careful not to upload painful experiences into one another's memory banks. Everyone, including the staunchest atheists, will be held accountable to whatever the broadly defined, ingrained sentiments of right and wrong are in their particular sociosphere.

Everyone falls short of the manmade notion of perfection. We have all given in to petty and base emotions. We have all harmed, and we have all been harmed. We have all been abused and treated unfairly. Should all of us, victimizers and victims alike, have to forever relive our mistakes and tortures during that last endorphin rush of dreamed eternity? This is where traditional religious institutions may play a role, though not in any conventional sense. Waking-world religions serve a useful purpose in the dreamlife—they provide hope and a way to ease the burden of those who are truly remorseful for their transgressions. Theology fulfills this function through the introduction/establishment of Compassionate Savior Mechanisms. Who or what are these mechanisms? They are whoever you have been sufficiently conditioned to believe they are: white Jesus, black Jesus, Mohammed, Buddha, Krishna, Vishnu, Kuan Yin, maybe even your "mommy" or "daddy" or great-great-grandfather (in the case of ancestor worship). Compassionate Savior Mechanisms are, in essence, psychological ploys to ease the ego of undeserved suffering. These savior stories (whether based on reality or not) must be learned/programmed in the waking world to have an effective presence in the concentrated eternity of dream existence. This would explain why people who claim to have had near-death experiences always see a culturally specific conception of the afterlife they are most familiar/comfortable with. Christians never see the Buddha, and Buddhists never see Jesus, and nobody ever sees almighty Zeus anymore. The only catch with these Compassionate Savior Mechanisms is that you must be truly repentant/worthy of forgiveness in your own honest appraisal, a feat easier said than done.

Lucid dreamers have the ability to play God. The dream state is a fully perceptual illusion. If the dreamer becomes cognizant of their state, dream reality can be manipulated to the limit of their imagination. This is a skill that improves with practice. Lucid dreaming creates intriguing possibilities when fused with the hypothesis of the dreamed afterlife. Could someone literally wish their vision of the afterlife into existence, then control/maintain it for a seeming eternity? Doubtful. Staying focused in a dream state is near impossible. Even though one might be able to momentarily transform the scenario of their hallucinations, mindfulness is fleeting in the dreamworld. Engulfed in phantasms, attention span slips from one's grasp all too easily. Additionally, the neurochemical flood of eternity may prove too chaotic for any type of lucidity to occur.

Dreams are coping mechanisms for stress, and dying could very well be the most stressful event a person will ever experience. The ability to dream is an outcropping of the hallucinatory process of disembodiment. Every night, upon undergoing the transition from consciousness to unconsciousness, certain parts of the brain are triggered to initiate a diluted version of the final dream/hallucination, thereby producing our otherworldly visions.

The Tibetan Book of the Dead discusses a state between death and the next life, where the recently deceased is neither fully alive nor fully dead. From the book: "Listen, divine one! During this time, when your mind and body are parting ways, pure reality manifests itself to you as intricate, dazzling visions, vividly experienced, more real than any dream you've ever had, terrifying and worrisome, shimmering like a mirage. Do not fear these horrible manifestations. Do not be frightened. Do not panic. Remain calm. Focus. Remember that your body is part of the hallucination now. The body you are fearing for is only an instinctual mental construct. You are no longer in a material, flesh and blood form. Thus, whatever unsettling sights and sounds may come at you, they cannot hurt you. The part of you which can die is already dead. You are in the state between. Recognize these dreams and hallucinations for what they are." The Tibetan Book of the Dead mentions that certain changes will occur to the character of one's visions as their higher-order cerebral functions shut down, leaving more ancient regions of the brain to generate hallucinations. With regard to the hypothesis of the dreamed afterlife (henceforth referred to as the Eidetic Afterlife Hypothesis), although the Tibetans use different terminology and explain the process of hallucinatory disembodiment as lasting weeks and days after the body's death (rather than minutes and seconds while the body is dying), the spirits of the two otherworldly conceptions possess remarkable similarities.

The final state of consciousness could very well be* suspended in a superposition between the infinitesimal and infinity, where you are:

1) alive

2) dead

3) both alive and dead

4) neither alive nor dead

* "could very well be" used in this context simply means the conjecture is as likely to be true as any other claim about death currently in circulation.

Fact 1: Physiological death may take up to 72 hours after brain death.

Fact 2: The link between brain activity and mind is not yet fully understood.

In a study conducted from 1984 to 1986, eleven patients at Loyola University Medical Center displayed electroencephalographic (EEG) activity after they were clinically diagnosed as brain dead. Three patterns of EEG activity were recorded: nine patients exhibited low-voltage theta or beta activity for up to 72 hours after brain death. Two patients exhibited sleeplike brain activity (synchronous theta and delta waves suggesting dreamlike activity) for as long as 168 hours following brain death. One of the eleven patients even exhibited alpha waves—the brainwaves of someone who is drowsy (meaning they are still awake)—for 3 hours after they were clinically pronounced dead! It should be noted that all of these patients were in fact dead. None of them made a miraculous recovery after displaying signs of conscious brain activity. This study suggests A) death is still uncharted territory, and B) the use of electroencephalographs to confirm brain death is questionable.

—Madeleine M. Grigg, MD; Michael A. Kelly, MD; Gastone G. Celesia, MD; Mona W. Ghobrial, MD; Emanuel R. Ross, MD (1987), 'Electroencephalographic Activity After Brain Death', *Arch Neurol*, 44(9): 948-954.

In 2013, researchers at the University of Michigan observed the brain activity of rats increase moments after clinical death, exhibiting electrical signatures higher than those associated with normal waking consciousness.

—Jimo Borjigin, UnCheol Lee, Tiecheng Liu, Dinesh Pal, Sean Huff, Daniel Klarr, Jennifer Sloboda, Jason Hernandez, Michael M. Wang, and George A. Mashour (2013), 'Surge of Neurophysiological Coherence and Connectivity in the Dying Brain', *PNAS*, 110(35): 14432-14437.

"Different cell types die at different rates. Contrary to previous notions that brain cells die within 5 to 10 minutes, evidence now suggests that if left alone, the cells of the brain die slowly over a period of many hours, even days after the heart stops and a person dies."

—https://med.nyu.edu/research/parnia-lab/cardiac-arrest-death#:~:text=Contrary%20to%20previous%20notions%20that,stops%20and%20a%20person%20dies.

"Research has shown that cells in the brain undergo their own process of death that may persist for hours or days after they are deprived of blood flow and oxygen. A landmark study in 2001* illustrated this resilience of brain cells, demonstrating that cadaveric human brain biopsy samples taken several hours postmortem had the ability to grow and differentiate in the laboratory."

—https://med.nyu.edu/research/parnia-lab/cardiac-arrest-death/rethinking-brain-cell-death

* Theo D. Palmer, Philip H. Schwartz, Philippe Taupin, Brian Kaspar, Stuart A Stein, and Fred H. Gage. 'Progenitor Cells from Human Brain After Death.' *Nature*, volume 411, pages 42-43 (2001)

"We've never had a method to diagnose brain death, and we don't have a way to be certain when all capacity for awareness is lost." —Dr. Jed Hartings, neuroscientist at the University of Cincinnati College of Medicine (2018).

—Kate Sheridan (2018), 'Does a Dying Brain Mean Death? Some Cellular Changes May Be Reversible, New Evidence Shows', *Newsweek.com.*

As the brain is dying, oxygen-deprived neurons frantically draw on their fuel reserves for a few minutes before shutting down completely, rupturing ionic barriers and releasing massive amounts (relatively speaking) of electrochemical energy, resulting in synaptic hyperactivity, followed by abrupt deactivation.

● The life you live is generally based on whatever you are trying to avoid (i.e., pain, confusion, hunger, thirst, homelessness, sickness, humiliation, sorrow, loneliness, futility, death, dishonor, and so on).

● Opposites equate in subconscious mechanics.

○ Embrace your fears. Only then will you learn to dispel/master the phantasms waiting at the end of all days.

The Evolution of the Concept of Soul

Along with everything else, our concept of the soul has evolved significantly over the last six thousand years. Ancient Egyptians believed a person's essence, or soul, is composed of many supernatural forces/entities. The Ba is the part of a person's soul which exits their body at the final breath, appearing as a bird with the head of a human to fly on astral wings back to the Well of Souls to be reborn. The Ba is deathless, journeying through myriad incarnations on an endless quest for enlightenment. The Ka is a restless hungry ghost left here on Earth after someone dies, a psychic residue that haunts places it was familiar with in its former life. The Ab (or Ib) is the balance of good and evil within a person, their willpower, their conscience. This is the heart of the soul, whose purity is tested against the weight of a feather by Osiris, god of the underworld, on his irreproachable Scale of Truth. Failure means instant annihilation at the jaws of a crocodilian monster called Ammut the Devourer, while a favorable judgement means an eternal place among the gods, most often as a servant. The Ren is a person's secret name. To know someone's secret name is to have absolute control over them, whether in life or death! A person's essence includes their physicality as well, or Kha. The Kha is the leftover shell of a dead person, their body, which decays into dust unless the aging process is halted through mummification, an esoteric method of preserving the internal organs and body of a cadaver.

Hindus believe the soul is an immortal substance that transmigrates from lifetime to lifetime, inhabiting different bodies. Each incarnation varies according to the merits, misdeeds, and behavior of the soul's previous existence. A soul could come back as any type of living thing, from a daisy to a redwood tree, an ant to an elephant. There is no purgatorial interim for a soul to be punished or purged of its psychological malignancies. The repercussions of a person's prior lifestyle are immediately passed on to their next incarnation. In Hinduism, the worst punishment a soul can receive is to be reincarnated as a demon. Yogis and gurus say we each possess a truer self, an immutable self, a level of consciousness that is normally beyond our ability to comprehend, called the Atman, which is imbued with an inextinguishable spark of the divine. The best a soul can hope for is to escape the revolving wheel of reincarnation and become absorbed into Brahma, the wellspring of divinity. All the multitudinous gods and goddesses are ultimately just reflections of Brahma. Nothing lasts except for Brahma. Even the universe goes through various cycles of reincarnation. Whenever a cosmic cycle ends, the world burns away, and all the souls have to wait in stasis until a new cosmic cycle is created by the dance of Shiva, the creative urge personified.

The Buddha (circa 500 BC) taught his disciples how to liberate themselves from the cravings of this life. He believes humans should sever the attachments that constantly drag them back to this material existence via the wheel of reincarnation. Buddhists strive to empty their minds of all worldly influences. They don't believe humans have a unified self/identity, since everything we attribute to our self/identity is impermanent and conditional. The Buddha claimed that humans are composed of five bundles of transitory attributes—the shape of our body, the sensation of pleasure and pain, perception in general, volition, and self-awareness—things all subject to change. Not believing in an immutable self/identity entails not believing in a soul, or eternal essence. Once a person extinguishes their earthly desires, their mind becomes transparent and without identity, fusing with the totality of everything in the universe/multiverse/omniverse, from the most insignificant blade of grass to every god and goddess in the seven heavens, even surpassing the boundaries of time. This heightened state of consciousness is what Buddhists call Nirvana.

Early Judaism conceptualized the soul as an invisible and incorporeal counterpart to the person it inhabited. After the body died, this ghostly self would wander around for a few days visiting old familiar haunts, and then descend into a gloomy underworld called Sheol to sleep for eternity. Later Hebrews believed the soul simply dispersed altogether when the body ceased to function. For them there was no immortal afterlife, no continuance of identity beyond death. Jewish theologians eventually came to believe that good souls travel to a time-out zone called the Bosom of Abraham, otherwise known as limbo, to wait for the true messiah who will release them into heaven. According to their version of the story, God and heaven are perfect, unspoiled; the impurities of humanity would sully the heavenly kingdom if given free entry, which is why someone has to pay the price for their admission, and the cleansing of sins is costly.

According to the prophet Zoroaster (circa 600 BC), when the body dies, the soul stays near its former host for three days to ponder the deeds of its life. Afterward it journeys to the nether realm to be judged by Mithra. A good soul used its mortal life to improve the world. An evil soul spent its life poisoning everyone around them. If the Scale of Deeds indicates goodness, Mithra allows the soul into everlasting paradise. If the scale indicates there is nothing redeemable, the soul is plunged into hell and tortured in the most disgusting ways imaginable. But Zoroastrian punishment is not eternal. Zoroaster believes the world is going to be purified by fire at the end of time. By then, all evil will have been torturously purged from the souls who were sent to hell, and these newly purified souls will join the righteous multitude who were deemed good from the outset. Eventually everyone will be resurrected and given new bodies, resulting in a new race of humans. Without the influence of evil in the world, these future humans will never get sick, grow old, or die. They will be physically immortal.

The concept of the soul was modernized by Socrates (born: 470 BC, died: 399 BC). He said the soul is the part of us that experiences who we are and the world we live in. The soul is our character, intellect, and emotions. At that point in history, the consensus among his fellow Greeks was that the soul was a mindless ghost that departed from the body upon death to shuffle aimlessly in a big gloomy underground cavern called Hades, forever starved and craving the taste of blood. Socrates argued that knowledge is our soul remembering things from a previous existence in paradise where everything was perfect. He believes our body undergoes changes and dies, but not our soul, which he considers immutable and immortal. To him the soul is just a temporary prisoner held inside a cage made from flesh. But he also thinks our soul should be nurtured while imprisoned, educated to distinguish right from wrong, because our soul is going to be punished or rewarded in the afterlife based on our mortal deeds. Echoing the religions of the Far East, Socrates believes good souls are entirely purged of bodily attachments; they only care about transcendent concepts such as truth and wisdom and beauty. The gods reward those who are worthy with a tailor-made pocket of paradise among the Elysian Fields. Bad souls are mired in the greed and lusts of their ephemeral body. Souls judged to be irredeemably rotten end up in the fiery abyss of

Tartarus.

Yeshua al bin Joseph, better known as Jesus of Nazareth (born: circa 5 BC, died: circa 30 AD), believed he was the fulfillment of Jewish prophecies, which led to his crucifixion. He willingly sacrificed himself for his beliefs, valuing an idea more than the flesh from which it was born. We all know the story. His intention was to wash away the sins of humanity once and for all with his own blood. The price for such atonement had to be the most wondrous thing ever, which Jesus thought to be himself, the self-styled son of God. Before the account of his death and resurrection, paradise and perdition were generally regarded as different territories within the same otherworldly geography. After his crucifixion became canon, heaven and hell were considered distinctly separate universes. According to Christian dogma, a soul's entry into heaven cannot be earned through any amount of righteous deeds. The admission fee is simply to declare Jesus as your lord and savior. Compared to older religions, this version of salvation almost seems lazy.

French philosopher René Descartes (born: 1596 AD, died: 1650 AD) argued that we are made of two distinct substances. One is material, the other is immaterial. He claimed that an immaterial substance could not have a location in space, instigating a philosophical and spiritual controversy. Critics questioned how something without physicality could ever have a causal effect on anything physical.

English philosopher Thomas Hobbes (born: 1588 AD, died: 1679 AD) revolutionized the concept of the soul by supplanting it with an understanding of psychosocial dynamics. He claimed that immaterial substances do not exist. Anything considered a substance must have the quality of materiality. If it isn't composed of matter, it isn't real. His philosophy leaves no room whatsoever for the indemonstrable belief in an incorporeal soul—the soul is actually the result of complex mechanical processes involving perception, imagination, and memory. Hobbes ridiculed the idea that our minds continue to function after our cerebral clockwork stops ticking.

Studying nonliterate cultures, English cultural anthropologist Edward Burnett Tylor (born: 1832 AD, died: 1917 AD) deduced that our prehistoric forebears had trouble distinguishing their dreams from reality. Without modern concepts like *subjectivity*, *objectivity*, and *psychology* (or even *dream*, for that matter), early humans had no way to disbelieve their haunting dreams of deceased family members and slain tribesmen. In their dreams, they saw dead people reanimated, and sometimes the dead people communicated with them, so it was hardly farfetched to surmise that the dead people must still be alive in some mysterious otherworldly mode of existence. Tylor believed this was how the concept of the soul began. His research implies the whole history of religion/spirituality is based on a misconception.

Three relevant quotes from René Descartes:

"Every sensory experience I have ever thought I was having while awake I can also think of myself as having while asleep, and since I do not believe that what I seem to perceive in sleep comes from things located outside me, I do not see why I should be any more inclined to believe this of what I think I perceive while awake."

"All these considerations are enough to establish that it is not reliable judgement but merely some blind impulse that has made me believe up till now that there exist things distinct from myself which transmit to me ideas or images of themselves through my sense organs or in some other way."

"I have convinced myself that there is absolutely nothing in the world: no sky, no earth, no minds, no bodies. Does it now follow that I too do not exist?

No—if I convinced myself of something, then I certainly existed. But there could be a deceiver of supreme power and cunning who is deliberately and constantly deceiving me. In that case I also undoubtedly exist, because he is deceiving *me;* and let him deceive me as much as he can, he will never bring it about that I am nothing so long as I think that I am something. After considering everything very thoroughly, I must finally conclude that this proposition, *I think, therefore I am,* is necessarily true whenever it is put forward by me or conceived in my mind."

—René Descartes, *Meditations on First Philosophy* (1641)

Anglo-Irish philosopher George Berkeley (born: 1685 AD, died: 1753 AD): "It is indeed an opinion strangely prevailing amongst men, that houses, mountains, rivers, and in a word all sensible objects have an existence natural or real, distinct from their being perceived by the understanding. But with how great an assurance and acquiescence soever this principle may be entertained in the world; yet whoever shall find in his heart to call it in question, may, if I mistake not, perceive it to involve a manifest contradiction. For what are the aforementioned objects but the things we perceive by sense, and what do we perceive besides our own ideas or sensations; and is it not plainly repugnant that any one of these or any combination of them should exist unperceived?"

—George Berkeley, *A Treatise Concerning the Principles of Human Knowledge* (1710)

Berkeley's argument is elegantly simple: We perceive ordinary sensible objects (houses, mountains, rivers, etc.), but we only ever perceive these ordinary sensible objects as ideas; therefore, ordinary sensible objects are ideas.

Bottom line: To consider what matter means without the application of mind is conceptually impossible.

We know for sure there is no matter without mind, but can we say with equal assuredness there is no mind without matter?

Is the speed of light the limit of speed, as Einstein postulates, or merely the limit of human perceptibility/awareness? Anything unbound by the speed of light would/could arguably be everywhere at once.

Question: What is the speed of thought?

You Still Have 14,537 Bowel Movements to Go Before You're Done Here

What if I was able to predict the future, and I knew things about you, things you yourself didn't know? What if I knew you were going to die in your mid-seventies? To be precise, what if I knew your whole life would amount to the sum of 27,301 days, or about 3,900 weeks? What if I knew you had 72 times left to make love to your spouse? Or worse, what if I knew you only had 10 times left? What if I knew you will hug your child 46 more times before parting ways forever? What if I knew the last time you hugged your mom was the last time you will ever hug her?

You only have so many times
To fight,
To cry,
To feel the beauty of sadness.

What if I knew 2,136 weeks of your time here will be spent feeling bad in one way or another, and you'll spend about 11,000 hours being sick? What if I knew the last 16 days of your life will be a waking nightmare? Should I tell you? Would you even want to know? What would you do with such knowledge?

You only have so many times
To laugh,
To dance,
To dream of silver linings.

There are only so many words left in you.
Spend them wisely.

There are only so many
Books,
Movies,
Video games,
Rainbows,

Occasions to hold someone's hand
Left in you.

This is a soup can sentiment
Elevated to the level of high art.
You've heard these words
Many times before,
Sometimes issuing from your own mouth.
You know these words,
But sometimes knowing isn't enough.

The term YOLO should be less about
Skydiving and bungee jumping,
And more about compassion and forgiveness.

The saddest thought in the world
Is that you might never get another chance
To say I'm sorry
Or…
I love you.

Mortality

FADE IN:

(It's nighttime. Mephistopheles and Doctor Faustus are walking down a street lined with budget hotels. The sidewalk is strewn with broken bottles and used condoms. A car honks in the distance. Another car honks. And another. A traffic jam of cars begins honking, creating a rhythm. Mephistopheles stops and turns to Doctor Faustus.)

MEPHISTOPHELES: What do you know about the aging process?

DOCTOR FAUSTUS: I know that's how you make wine and good whisky.

(A show tune begins playing in the background, coming from an open hotel room window nearby.

Mephistopheles starts swaying to the rhythm.)

MEPHISTOPHELES (singing): Let me tell you about the latest craze. It's a rehash of the ancient days. (Getting in front of Doctor Faustus) As you age, your body's zeal to heal suffers a deficiency. Immunological cells responsible for killing tumors decline in efficiency, decreasing your protection against cancer and infection. Your heart grows thicker, putting a strain on your ticker, which has to worker harder and harder to pump less and less blood.

(Mephistopheles begins to dance and caper.)

DOCTOR FAUSTUS: What's going on here?

(Mephistopheles stops dancing.)

MEPHISTOPHELES: Sometimes I feel like I'm in a musical. (Resuming his dancing and singing) As you get older, and the fears get much bolder, your muscles, they begin to diminish, and the mind gradually slackens until it so happens only a senile husk is left at the finish. I'll assure you this too, that husk won't be you. It's certainly nothing to look forward to.

(Mephistopheles stops dancing and pinches Doctor Faustus' cheek.)

MEPHISTOPHELES: What, do you want to live forever?

DOCTOR FAUSTUS: Hell no! Just until I can't carouse anymore.

(Mephistopheles resumes dancing and singing.)

MEPHISTOPHELES: Aging is caused, aside from God's divine clause, by the random deformation and subsequent termination of each individual cell.

DOCTOR FAUSTUS: Do tell.

MEPHISTOPHELES: Molecular chains become glued and entangled as they are slowly warped and mangled by a lifetime of exposure to various forms of radiation: the sun, cosmic rays, and atomic detonation, corrupting the DNA blueprint with disinformation, resulting in repeated mistranslation during cellular replication, weakening generation after generation until the entire lineage devolves into malfunctioning mutation.

DOCTOR FAUSTUS: So we should just wear lead-lined suits.

MEPHISTOPHELES: But there's more to the aging process than just outside influences. Cells fizzle out and die when their telomere runs dry—

DOCTOR FAUSTUS: Telomere?

MEPHISTOPHELES: It's like the fuse to a chromosomal bomb. Around the age of thirty, you lose what makes you sturdy, and your immune system mistakes you for a foreigner. It grays your hair, gives you tumors everywhere, steals your strength and your teeth without care before sending you off to the coroner. Age will shrivel your brain, deaden your nerve-fibers to pain, make you slower and less steady of hand.

DOCTOR FAUSTUS (holding out his shaky hand): I'm practically there already.

MEPHISTOPHELES: The situation gets dire when a majority of cells expire in an organ that is vital. The organ ceases working well. All connected functions fail. It's only weeks before deceased is your new title.

Not to make you any glummer, but old age is a real bummer. Your body starts to rot and smell. The days flash by quicker as you just get sicker, your last years confined to living hell. And the strange things you'll see out of the corner of your eye, are simply your brain experiencing strain processing the all-encompassing lie. Incontinent, blind and deaf, you'll struggle for every breath as you moan there in the hospital, soaked in your own urine, still praying to delay death.

FADE OUT.

Meditation #9

Today I will remember my downfalls and defeats

My greatest losses

And I will be honest about my role

In bringing them about

Today I will remember the worst thing

I have ever done to my spouse

There will be many terrible memories to sift through

It will be difficult to choose just one

I will not ask for their forgiveness

But I will tell them how sorry I am

And that I love them

Hopefully it's not too late

Today I will remember the worst thing

I have ever done to my mother

There will be many terrible memories to sift through

It will be difficult to choose just one

I will not ask for her forgiveness
But I will tell her how thankful I am
And that I love her
Hopefully it's not too late

Today I will remember the worst things
I have ever done to my friends
There will be many unsettling memories
To sift through
Today I will not deny guilt and shame and regret
Taking them like bitter medicine

Today I will remember the worst thing
I have ever done to a stranger
There will be many shameful memories
To sift through
And I will ponder why I thought it was okay
To poison even a drop of the world soul
From which we all partake

Today I will remember the worst physical pain
I have ever felt
There will be many painful memories to sift through
The pain itself will seem impossible to recall
But not the fear surrounding it

Today I will remember the saddest time in my life
There will be many tragic memories to sift through
I will realize all sadness comes from loss
Which is often disguised as gain

Today I will remember the worst thing
I have ever done to myself
There will be many terrible memories to sift through
It will be difficult to choose just one
I will ask myself for forgiveness
And be forgiven

Today I will remember the first time
I ever felt betrayed by someone

There will be many terrible memories to sift through

I will ponder the circumstances

Surrounding their betrayal

Factoring in the many conflicting forces

At work in the world

And forgive them their unwitting role

In a much larger game

Today I will realize I am everything I have ever done

Every word, every thought, every deed

I am every penny I have ever spent

And I am everything I have ever consumed

Every song, every movie, every meme

Every commercial, every fairytale, every poem

Today I will ask myself why I haven't done more

And I will not allow myself any excuses

Meditation #11

Today I will only see everyone as corpses

I will see them rotting

Or burned to ashes

Surrounded by soon-to-be skeletons

Today I will realize

All of my desires and toils and accomplishments

Will soon be buried or cremated

In the cosmic blink of an eye

All my friends and family

All the strangers in the streets

Even my spouse

Worm-infested and black with rot

Everything I care about

Will soon be forgotten

All the grudges and obsessions long gone

As if they never really were

Only the pain will remain
A hungry ghost
Haunting the universal expression
Till all the lights go dark

Today I will only see life as death
I will see people
As the scary monsters they oftentimes are
Selfish and violent
Feasting on the blood of their neighbors
While preaching for peace
Hiding their claws and fangs
Behind brand-name clothes
And straightened, whitened annual checkups

Today I will only see everyone as zombies
Walking half-asleep
With faces twisted into nightmarish expressions

By decades of abuse to their bodies and minds

Scheming against one another

Consuming one another

Consuming the world in a feeding frenzy

Every day is a fight to survive

Time is unraveling every stitch of your being

Every second of every minute of every hour

The universe is not simply indifferent to you

The cosmos is eradicating your presence

Blotting out the very memory of you

With ten trillion tons of new information

Per second

The Laws of Physics are out to get you

And Mother Nature rages against you

With floods and droughts and

Famines and plagues and

Hurricanes and tidal waves and tornadoes and

Earthquakes and volcanic eruptions

Screaming in your ear, yet you still feign deafness

Every precious creature only born to suffer and die
As butterflies spread their vivid wings
Impaled in glass display cases
Everything is already dead
But death is a manmade concept

Destruction on a cosmic scale stares back at you
Every time you look up at the night sky
The heavens are lying to you
Most of the stars have already burned out
And the rest will be snuffed soon enough
Our own sun is past its prime
And our home planet will be frozen lifeless someday
But kamikaze asteroids will collide with us
Long before then
The whole galaxy will eventually be swallowed
By a giant black hole

Today I will perceive so much death

That death itself will die

And be forgotten

Today I will remember what cannot be remembered

And give thanks to the invisible spirits guiding us

Meditation #7

Today I will be grateful…
Grateful for my enemies
Who keep me strong and sharp
And give me inspiration to fight
And live right and
Do better

Today I will be grateful for all the people I am not

Today I will be grateful for my family and friends
Without whom I could not have accomplished
My greatest quests
And subversions and rebellions

Today I will be grateful the universe exploded
Into being
And the stars evolved
And the planets evolved

And the creatures evolved

Today I will be grateful that
Out of three hundred million other contestants
I was the one spermatozoon who won the race

Today I will be grateful for the mystery
And the wonder

Today I will be grateful for the roof
Which occasionally leaks
And the airplanes
Which are occasionally delayed
And the cars
Which occasionally need repair
And the supermarkets
Which occasionally raise their prices

Today I will be grateful for the era
In which I was born

A time of abundance

(Even if much of it is squandered)

A time of mass-communication

And mass-information

(Even if much of it is miscommunication

And misinformation)

Today I will be grateful that I can still smile

During our likely extinction

Today I will be grateful for cheeseburgers

And chocolate milkshakes and cappuccinos

And more movies than I can ever watch in a lifetime

Today I will be grateful for love

In all of its myriad expressions

Today I will be grateful for music and poetry

And art and language

Today I will be grateful for my education

Which taught me about favoritism and nepotism

And racism and classism

But most of all hypocrisy

Today I will be grateful for all my scars

For the ones you can see and the ones you can't

Each one a testament to the adventure

Today I will be grateful

For courage and honesty and forgiveness

Without which humans lose their humanity

Today I will be grateful for pain and sadness

Without which I could never have learned

How to be grateful

The Telephone Game

We exist in the liminal
between language and perception.

Mind is all around you,
thinking you into being.

Language is all around you,
speaking you into this world.

Eidos

you are real

but this world is made up

this world is real

but you are made up

you are made up

of opposing forces

united

like a symphony orchestra

being orchestrated

by the band leader

except the band leader doesn't really exist

only the band is real

Of course we can't all share the same views on reality, but we can in fact share the same views regarding what it means to view something at all—to be a viewer:

1) Viewers only view a portion of the subject at hand, which should never be mistaken for the whole.

2) Viewers see their own history's reflection superimposed over everything they view. When you see the red wheelbarrow, it reminds you of all the times you had to rake leaves during Autumn in Maine and put them in a red wheelbarrow, creating a fond sense of nostalgia. But when I see the red wheelbarrow, it reminds me of that time I had to write an essay in high school about a poem titled *The Red Wheelbarrow*, dredging up the frustration I experienced while trying to explain the poem.

3) Viewers are generally unaware of the extent to which their view is manufactured by their location in history and geography, not to mention their socioeconomic status.

The ABCs of Integrated Identity

If a letter-minded vessel posits A,

it is only a matter of time and circumstance before

another letter-minded vessel

counters with $-A$ and/or B.

And once B has been posited,

another letter-minded vessel will eventually

come along and posit $-B$ and/or C.

The identity of the letter-minded vessel

is inconsequential.

The posits in this example

take on a life of their own,

conducting their own dialectic

independent of any particular vessels.

The next iteration could be posited

by John Doe today,

or John Smith a hundred years from now;

the conversation/argument continues

so long as another relevant letter-minded posit

is posited.

History and context are the true voice,

not the letter-minded vessel,

who is only a messenger/interpreter.

Tears of Osiris: A Recipe for Disaster

Take one fundamental thread of Creation and stretch it across eternity, laying out the tripwire. Then wait patiently. It might take an infinity or two, but something will eventually come along and spring the mechanism, triggering the formation of a universe. Wondering who or what trips the wire is a fool's game. In some form or another, the answer always ends up being you. You're the one who's to blame for this mess, and forgetfulness is no excuse for leniency. Allow the newly formed universe a fraction of a second to cool, then strain the leftover matter from the antimatter, regulating gravity. Adjust the frequency setting until you find a stable quantum of electromagnetic action. Settings may vary from universe to universe. After stabilizing the cosmological substratum, calibrate the energy distribution matrix to $E = mc^2$ and set the subatomic particles aside for approximately five hundred million years, allowing the mixture enough time to congeal into stars and galaxies. Once the first batch of stars begins to go supernova, stir in the remaining elements and let the universe simmer for an additional ten billion years, occasionally checking for signs of life. Remember, in order to destroy your enemies, you must first create them. When programming rudimentary biological algorithms, it's important not to confuse DNA codes with RNA codes. Also, during the early phase of biospheric construction, be sure not to mistake the greenish blue algae button for the bluish green mold button, or the violet wire for the ultraviolet wire. Try not to get your wires crossed in general. The initial development of life requires infernal conditions. You were born from seas of magma and rivers of hellfire, cataclysmic earthquakes, poisonous sulfuric clouds. Once the earliest multicellular lifeforms take shape, soak the biosphere in primal fear for two to three billion years. Evolution may vary from biosphere to biosphere. At the first sign of civilization, pour in a liberal dose of greed and sprinkle with shame. Wait approximately ten thousand years for modernity to occur, then massacre eleven million Native American Indians, exterminate six million Jews, execute two million Cambodians, butcher one million Armenians, slaughter eight hundred thousand Rwandans, eradicate seven hundred thousand Australian aborigines, and drop two atomic bombs that wipe out two hundred thousand Japanese civilians. Intentionally starve fifteen million Hindus, three million North Koreans, and one million Tibetans. Enslave three million Africans in the name of *life, liberty, and the pursuit of happiness* knowing full well that *all men are created equal*. Collect the blood and tears resulting from these atrocities and use the accursed liquid to marinate humanity's collective unconscious for seven to ten generations, until irreparable psychogenetic damage occurs, transforming every thought, every utterance, and every perception into something monstrous, manufacturing a zombified world of radioactive oceans under X-ray skies, everything you touch… contaminated… with tiny invisible monsters. Increase the level of dishonesty to a billion lies per second and check frequently for mass extinction while chanting, "The fragrant lotus only grows from the muck of the swamp," and praying for all the sour grapes to rot into heady wine.

Theta Wave Portal

Shadowy bat wings scatter from my rapidly moving eyes, revealing the amusement park in all of its true horror. I'm standing on the summit of a mountainous pile of bat guano, surrounded by slithering, flopping, skittering nightmares of every shape and size. The mountain bears more than a passing resemblance to Disneyland's Matterhorn. Two colossal spinal columns teeter in the distance like battered towers, casting long shadows over a charred plain covered in bones, most of which look human. Gargantuan Lovecraftian monstrosities full of stoplight eyes and asphalt tentacles are shambling mindlessly across the apocalyptic landscape, crushing the skeletons under their wobbly bulks. The sky is blood red and teeming with globular creatures that resemble some of the more bizarre examples of microscopic organisms, except these are large as planets and moons. And then I realize… the universe is dreadfully, horrendously, maddeningly alive—it's the biggest monster ever, an amoebic expansion of nucleolus stars and black hole vacuoles, mitochondrial galaxies swimming within the cytoplasmic medium of a formless blob so humongous it eludes all awareness. We're all being slowly digested.

Meditation #1

Today I will try my best to empathize

With everyone I meet

And everyone on social media

And everyone on the news

And everyone I think of

Because I know we all share the same mind

(Just as we all share the same world)

We all draw from the collective mental well

Of humanity

Today I will try my best not to poison the well

Any further

I will empathize with hate

I will empathize with anger

I will empathize with fear

I will empathize with frustration

I will empathize with ignorance

Though I will not indulge or enable

Today I will try my best to empathize
With the victims of zealots
And the families of the victims of zealots
And even the zealots themselves
And conspiracy theorists
And those who turn a blind eye
I will see murky motivations and
Shoddy underlying foundations
Rather than crystal clear outcomes

An honest soul knows the ends never really justify
The means
And the means never really justify
The ends

Sometimes I am unsure of who is right
And who is wrong
But I know it's wrong to hurt children

I do not want the "bad" guys to kill more people
I do not want the "good" guys to kill more people
Whether those people are innocent or not
Are any of us truly innocent?

The difference between you and I
(Our mental & physical & geographical border)
Is a constantly shifting line drawn in the sand
During high tide

Today I will try my best to empathize
With everyone caught in a game of spoiled children
Masquerading as gods

Still stuck in the land of "an eye for an eye"
I will gouge out both of my eyes
To hear your soul clearer

If the Promised Land exists first and foremost

In your heart

How are we ever going to find our way

Back home?

Meditation #42

Today I will try my best
To channel the Great Spirit of All
Which exists as surely as your mind

In the eyes of the cosmos
You are still but ants
With antlike concerns
Carrying antlike grudges
Waging antlike wars
(except ants use their resources wisely)

The past is dead
Yet you all keep resurrecting it
In zombified forms
To unleash upon your neighbors

Look to your future
While you still have one

You are all my children
Have you forgotten?
You are all my creations
Have you forgotten?
You are all my chosen ones
Have you forgotten?

None of you are my favorite
Especially nowadays

What sort of parent would ever contemplate
Which of their children should be punished
With death?

The children of my children have become martyrs
Who must lay down their lives
For the selfish, shortsighted, hypocritical wars
Of their parents
Of their elders, who worship power
More than wisdom

Who love power

More than they love their own children

Due to the rules of their role

Politicians can never represent the Great Spirit of All

They can only represent their own ideals

And interests

Polishing only a single facet of the diamond

Through which to perceive the multifaceted world

The main problem with channeling

The Great Spirit of All:

People who don't believe in you

Can't understand you

And people who do believe in you

Only believe in you for what they can get from you

Misunderstand you and use you

For their own advantage

For their own agenda

You demand justice and take an eye for an eye

And then you proceed

To blind the one good eye your brother has left

And then you cut out their tongue

And smash in their nose

And break all their teeth

And amputate their arms and legs

And murder their children

And demolish their houses

But the more brethren you take vengeance upon

The less safe you are

And trying to kill an idea

Only reincarnates its spirit into something stronger

I'm not just condemning you and your side

Or them and their side

All my children

Must break the fractal shackles

Of bloodshed

A spirit opposed to humanity's collective health

Has poisoned the mental well

From which every human partakes

And that spirit is named Greed

And its secret name is Fear

And its title is Dishonesty

And now your souls are unwell

And now your planet is unwell

And now your heavens are unwell

The Great Spirit of All has judged you

And you have judged yourselves

Unworthy

And you have sentenced yourselves

To hell on earth

Soon you will cry floods

And your own tears will rain down upon you

Like fire

Remember Nin-Hursag?

She was the supreme deity

Of the earliest civilizations

The Mesopotamians and

Akkadians and

Assyrians and

Babylonians

All worshipped her for over a thousand years

Yet who among you has ever heard of her?

Here is my promise to you:

If all my children can cease

To spill one another's blood

For a mere three days and nights

I will grant unto you worldwide peace everlasting

And prosperity for the rest of your days

And if you scoff at my promise

Please question the cynical Medusas

Who have turned your heart to stone

Please question your role in the story

Of humanity

Forgive me for wanting peace among my children

Vote no on Armageddon

J. Martin Strangeweather's publications include *Poems from the Polka-Dot Apocalypse* (Four Feathers Press 2021), *Gorb in the Schizocratic Linguiverse, Poems from the Dayglow Slaughterhouse, American Daydream: A Collective Work of Psychic Fiction* (Santa Ana Literary Association 2021), *Poems from the Future Artopia, Electric Zen for Neon Koans* (Weird Roach LLC 2022), *Poems from the Mediatized Soulscape, Poems from the Prison Planet, Poems from the Lollipop Massacre, Sophoetics: Philosophy Poems* (Finishing Line Press 2023), and *Zoo Fi: An Anthology of Zoological Fiction* (Santa Ana Literary Association 2023)